RESOLUTIONS

Resolutions

An Erotic Poetry Collection

Micky Omega

Copyright © 2025 Micky Omega All rights reserved

No part of this book may be reproduced, or stored in a retrieval system, or transmitted in any form or by any means, electronic, mechanical, photocopying, recording, or otherwise, without express written permission of the publisher.

Imprint: Independently published

Cover design by: Micky Omega

TABLE OF CONTENTS

I: New Kinks..1
II: Vers Card..3
III: Slut...4
IV: Masturbation..6
V: Porn..8
VI: Erotica..9
VII: Collaboration...10
VIII: Dancing...12
IX: Self-Portrait..13
X: Slime...15
XI: Cage..16
XII: Cum Dump..17
XIII: Dildo..18
XV: Pup Play..21

XVI: Gaming	23
XVII: Orgasms	24
XVIII: 52 Weeks	26
XIX: Compliments	28
XX: Please Me	30
XXI: Face Card	32
XXII: Eating Ass	34
XXIII: Gayer	35
XXIV: Orgy	37
XXV: Parody	38
XXVI: Skirt	39
XXVII: Shaving	40
XXVIII: Cosplay	41
XXIX: DMs	43
XXX: Vanilla	44
XXXI: Doggy Style	45
XXXII: Pits	47
XXXIII: Punishment	48
XXXIV: Grand Canyon	49
XXXV: Nudes	50
XXXVI: Throat Fuck	52
XXXVII: Painting	54
XXXVIII: Poetry	55
XXXIX: Role Play	56
XL: I Love You	57
XLI: I Hate You	58
XLII: Swing	59
XLIII: Step on Me	60
XLIV: Holidays	61
XLV: Toys	62

XLVI: Cinema	64
XLVII: Laundry	65
XLVIII: Nipples	66
XLIX: Mirror	68
L: Resolutions	70
About the Author	73

I: New Kinks

I will sink my hands into the ground in the yard,
fingers stabbing past the roots and rock,
cool dirt spilling out over my palms.

I'll engage that masculine urge at the beach
that results in all those mile deep potholes
flooded by the coming froth of waves.

I'm going to burrow into the earth until the sky
is a pinprick of blue above me and I am
surrounded by the dark, wet, and soft.

Stay in the hole, sweet boy, until running
your fingers over the sprinkling black
elicits a sigh of desire from your bones.

Let me find new kinks in the coming years,
new moans and pleasures to fall into
on my walks around the house of my body.

When it's my time to go, I want to look
in the eyes of whatever God might exist
and tell them how I found pleasure down every road.

I want to say I lived a life of ecstasy,
one where I found holy sex in so many strange spots
that I get to claim I lived a good fucking life.

Micky Omega

Let me learn the joy of someone cutting my hair,
of kneeling in front of them in the shower,
manscaping my man with the rain on my back.

Let me shiver while sticking my tongue
in a man's fuzzy navel filled with a shot
of alcohol threatening to spill over the counter.

Let me whimper without hearing a thing,
all senses cut off as I'm at the mercy
of a man I can trust with all of me.

There is good in this creation, I'll say to God
when I have learned to jerk off to new fantasies
I couldn't dream of before digging the hole.

Resolutions

II: Vers Card

I need to head to the Gay Licensing Department
over on 69th and Dorothy and apply for renewal
on my vers card. It's sat in my wallet for years
without much use since I graduated college.

The judgy twink behind the counter will lift
a well-trimmed eyebrow and ask how many times
this vers-bottom has actually sunk my cock
inside some other man. I want to tell him: many.

So this year I'm going to flip fuck into the dawn
with a pack of energy drinks fueling our thrusts
into each other. In the morning, our holes will ache
and our balls will need weeks to fill back up.

III: Slut

I'm a submissive good boy slut.
For someone who likes to say that,
I sure don't have enough sex.

I don't kiss enough men at midnight.
My legs don't open as a motel with an
always vacant room like they long to do.

This year I'll pull up Grindr and find pits
to dive into tongue first with all the graceful
greed of an Olympic swimmer.

The gay club will bump with hyperpop
and the *thwaps!* of thighs against my ass
as a drum machine adding more beats to the music.

I'll stop paying lip service and start serving
with my lips gliding up and down throbbing flesh
slick with spit and pre-cum.

Enough seed will flood my body
that I will become fertile, overflowing
with enough life for a new universe.

Resolutions

This is the year I will force my running brain
to take off his marathon shoes to enjoy the feel
of a worshiping mouth against my weary soles.

I am scared of sex, and yet it is one of the blessings
of life. What a fool I would be to deny myself.
This is the year I embrace beatification of sin.

Micky Omega

IV: Masturbation

Slow and steady wins the race, says the turtle.
My cock is only a turtle when it's extremely soft.

Pleasure is not a task to be checked off, says the turtle,
so there's no need to rush through it like a cop.

I will not waste time by sitting in my bed with porn
playing on my laptop, because elation is not a waste.

I am not a construction site, so there's no need
to jackhammer like I have a deadline to fulfill.

Slow down, says the turtle. He's a master at edging,
at staring down the cliffside to the churning waves below.

The shortest point to the water is to leap to the beach,
but there are flowers on the winding path down to the
sand.

I am going to massage my flesh with gentle fingers
wet with silicone lubrication slowly vanishing.

When I duet-moan with a man, there's no speeding.
Sex is not a race-car. I am providing pleasure.

Cum makes me smile. I love to make a partner shudder
and curl their toes, but orgasms are not that goal.

If you walk slow with the sun baking your back,
says the turtle, *the cool waters will be a stronger balm.*

Sex is beauty. To love someone is to want to fuck them

Resolutions

in a way that empties their head of anything else.

I will love myself more this year. It will be a full love
that requires shouting and shaking in my bed.

I deserve to sail west into the waves of the ocean
on my own boat amidst the churning, spewing white.

I will masturbate like a hike on a Tuesday afternoon
whose destination is less important than the breeze on my
        face.

There are a million things to do today and yesterday.
If I'm one of them, I should take my time.

After all, if you're going to all the trouble of fucking yourself,
you might as well remember why men always come back.

Micky Omega

V: Porn

People often mistake art and erotica
as two different things. Art is film,
literature, sculpture, music – you get the idea.
Erotica is content. It's slop and filth.
But porn is still film. Nude drawings are drawings.
Erotica is literature. Dildos are sculptures.
Websites and self-publishers restrict erotica
in ways they wouldn't any other genre
because they're prudes playing a game
of pretend that doesn't understand this is all
artifice. Sure, that's a real uncut cock
gaping the porcelain redhead twink's hole,
but they're actors. Baby, this is still playing.
NSFW art makes artistic and philosophical
arguments. *This is beautiful!* they declare.

I am a harsh defender of the arts. I own a riot
shield coated in shattering fractures. As such,
I ought to sit and watch the entire film. I can't
fast forward to the blowjob and skip to the end.
This art demands watching with a hand on my
cock with it and my ears at attention. I will read
the credits of the gaffers and the editors and applaud
them on their job well done. My eyes will remain
on the screen even when I'm covered in white.
I will comment on the things I love and compliment
their makers. That is what it means to love art.

VI: Erotica

My pen is going to leak like an uncut man
whose underwear drawer is filled with small stains.
It's wet will mark the pages of notebooks as mine
the way his loads paint my and my face as his.

You must be the kink you want to see out in the world.
If I'm going to jerk off more, then I need to give my
      cock
more fuel to fill the imagination of its throbbing head.
I must write unendingly like Hamilton did.

Hamilton defended the Constitution to his fellow
      Americans.
My writings will defend horniness and sex itself.
I will tell you what to desire and how to dream of it.
My pages say you will come but not alone.

Micky Omega

VII: Collaboration

Acting is about reacting, as they say.
It's all over TV and roundtable talks.
You can react to anything if you're alert
or paranoid enough, take your pick.

I am an actor trained for the stage.
Performance twitches in my fingers
and projects my voice across the room.
I miss the blaring lights of a soundstage.

Someone train a camera on my flesh
and document how someone might want me.
Let it add ten pounds to my sweet undying gluttony,
how I always kiss like I'm in love.

Would you memorize a script and rehearse it
in my hotel room, reciting lines as I blow you?
I want to make porn that you watch for the plot,
for the cinematography, the careful score of moans.

Let us be ambition personified. You'll thrust deep
inside my ass with a pace that earns you
an Oscar nomination. The way your load will leak
from me is how I'll get Supporting Actor.

Resolutions

Let us make more than love. We can fuck
in melancholy and hatred, too. We can cum
as an apology between two friends. We can moan
as though delivering a monologue.

There is no more settling left in me for this life.
I choose to evolve into a greedy creature
who will make it all. Intertwine your sculpture
fingers with mine and join me on screen.

VIII: Dancing

I haven't danced enough in my life.
It's like after college my feet got scared
of shuffling over sticky floors with changing lights.
I used to be the sort to Macarena at every song
while somehow slowly stripping 'til
I was nearly free in nudity,
skin painted purple in the twirling lights.

I want to feel strong fingers against my hips
like I am clay meant to be molded in the spinning
pottery wheel of a man grinding against my ass.
Take me to the club and turn me into a vase
meant to hold the flowers of your cock,
then bring me back to your room
and plant as many seeds as you can.

IX: Self-Portrait

Look in the mirror.

It's difficult to do, isn't it? To look,
really look, and keep your eyes soft.

I am on a royal mission chartered by the kings
of my past who have ordered me to stare
at the glass until I share their eyes.

The worst part about being an indie erotic artist
is how often you have to stare at your own body
while editing together footage. Would I jerk off
to me? I have set sail to learn how.

My eyes will traverse the waves down to my cock
and watch as it grows long at the thought of placing
it in my own mouth. If I could suck myself off, I would.
I would kiss the fat head and trace my tongue tip
over the pulsing vein on the top of the shaft.

How many hours could I lose
if I could kiss my own ass? Men love
my ass. The photos I take, they say,
don't do it any justice. I like holding it.
To ass-kiss yourself it to learn how to be kind
to the oceans of flesh and blood you inhabit.

Micky Omega

I'd fuck you, I'll tell my reflection
until I believe it, until I make molds
of my cock and my hole and ship them off
to some artisan to make dildos and pocket pussies
out of. I'll learn what it is to make love to myself,
to moan out my own name, to draw
honey from my lips.

Look in the mirror.

Resolutions

X: Slime

Gag me on your cock, sir.
Hold my nose down in your pubes
even as I start to make pathetic sounds.
Feel the way my throat spasms against
the burrowing tip of your pre-cumming head.
You put a towel on the floor for a reason.
I agreed to be a toy for you to masturbate
inside of, to ruin, to fill, to make yours.
When water wells in my eyes and snot spills
from my nostrils, throat slime will drip from your balls.
Chuckle at the cascading warmth over your length,
at the sounds of struggle and surrender as I learn
my happy place is with your leg bent over my head,
holding me down all the way on your godly erection.
Help me embrace submission and pleasure.
That's what I like to hear, you'll say.
Good boy. That's a good fucking boy.

XI: Cage

A lot of the best art is formed under heavy restriction,
like a metal chastity cage pulling at your sack
and stopping you from cumming in five seconds.

I don't care much for meter and rhyme, for forms
of a more formal variety. I like my verse like my cock:
free. Yet there is a cage that sits in a drawer by my bed.

Keys and locks make for sexy necklaces. My favorite
doms on gay social media wear them as fashion
statements that they're going to mess you up for good.

How much better of a poet would I be if I wore a cage?
How much gooder of a boy if it wasn't metaphorical,
if someone else held the key and I had to earn freedom?

I want to surrender my orgasms to you, to only cum
at your stimulation or with your permission.
I want you to wear my key on your neck.

Let me wake you with a whimpering tongue
under the sheets. When you're far away,
send a selfie with your necklace, proof that I'm still yours.

XII: Cum Dump

In the hotel room, a marker will hang
as a necklace and another as a belt.
Temporary tally mark tattoos will paint
my chest and my stomach, counting each
life I'll gain with every load dumped inside me
by the men called together to celebrate
my birthday or some other passing fancy
that calls for me to be center of attention,
the bank of devotion with a brain swimming
from pleasure, from knowing I can provide
such elation to so many one after another,
some at the same time, stomach swelling
with life, breaths tasting of cum for weeks
to come. The permanent marker isn't really
permanent. It'll wash off rather quickly, actually.
My man will help me into the shower
with his cock hard against my back
as he helps me wash. He'll add his load
to the shampoo in my hair, and I'll say
that I'm jealous it wasn't inside me.

Micky Omega

XIII: Dildo

My dildo, that neon pink vibrator
that photographs so horribly,
is a lonely man.

He spends weeks at a time by himself,
untouched, laying on top my nightstand,
cyclops eye watching my every move.

On those rare nights he is held, he vibrates
with excitement and noisy pleasure,
just to find himself shoved in latex.

This is the year I treat him better.
He deserves kisses and flesh-to-flesh contact,
humming deep inside my hole.

In the coming months, I'll come to him,
and in his eagerness to be of use,
he'll train me to be a better whore.

Maybe I'll suction-cup stick him to the shower
and let his mating dances milk a load
from my prostate without touching myself.

Resolutions

We'll watch porn together on my bed
like couples cuddle with movies,
Netflix and fucking chilling.

Why would I buy these tools of self-love
just to let them cry from loneliness?
No more, I say. No more.

XIV: Pocket Pussy

Shit, it's kind of embarrassing
to cum so quickly inside silicone
when out of the handful of times
I've pounded some good boy
in the ass, most of them I didn't
finish because I got so goddamn
bored. *How long can this go on?*
But in the tight embrace of a toy,
it only takes a minute. It's sort of funny,
to be gay and only cum on top
when buried inside a fake pussy.

I'll bury it under a mountain of pillows
and thrust into artificial lips as my own
are busy trembling out imagined names.
I'm going to learn how to last for an hour,
how to orgasm and keep working
like a good boy would to earthquake
my bottom's hole around my cock.
This toy is going to teach me
how to cum on command.

XV: Pup Play

Buy a new hood since the one
with blue accent still smells
like chemicals a year later.

Baby book find a name to fill
a bone-shaped dog tag
declaring I am Pup ___.

Bend my neck for a thick
neoprene collar he can hold
while he guides my tongue to his taint.

Bark when he clips a leash
to the back and walk around
the room on all fours.

Learn how to slip into that mythical place
the people on Reddit call pup space
where you can play and just *be*.

Stick a plug in my hole with a tail
stuck out the end so it can wag
as I slobber on a bone.

Micky Omega

Pant in the wind like I've rediscovered
the amazement of blurring trees
and my face in the gentle breeze.

Play, baby boy.
Rediscover happiness
and slip into brand new barking joy.

XVI: Gaming

There are dreams that inspire,
like those who long to be doctors,
whose fingers grow calluses on guitar strings,
who study through the night to pass the bar,
who splatter themselves in paint,
who nurse sparring bruises in the night,
who long to create or heal or strive.

Then there are dreams like mine.
If you sat me down and asked
what I most desire at this very moment,
I'd say I want a nerdy man, a gaymer,
who will sit in a leather chair and say
shit like *AFK* into that dorky headset
sat on his face. He'll be mowing down mobs
of aliens or Linking Zelda up with Pikachu
or whatever it is gamers do. I'll be on my knees
between him and his screen, polishing
his Master Sword with my lips.

My dream is to kiss him between matches,
to bounce on his lap with his cock in my ass
while he rolls on some anime gacha game DPS
like my hole is the thing that brings him luck.

My dream is not so grand, and likely not
inspiring. Still, it's worthy of striving.
This year I will find it true.

XVII: Orgasms

There are 365 days in a year
if you're to believe Big Calendar.
It's almost poetic, in a way, like the universe
says, *You have a year to come full circle*
like a narrative with parallels between
the opening legs and the denouement.

Those five extra degrees seem to say,
though, that it's not enough to find
your way back to who you are.
For a year to be lived in, you must
take at least a single extra step
beyond the 360, beyond mere narrative.

If I am going to walk around and even forward
after, then I need stumble through self-love
and stop spiraling around all the old things
I'm caught up on. There are 365 days,
so I ought to love myself to completion
at least 365 times this year.

I will spill so much seed to the earth
that they'll write folklore about me,
the long awaited sequel to Johnny Appleseed,
that notorious breeder of thick assed bottoms.
I will be the alpha Omega in that I will be
the one to greedily grab at happiness.

Resolutions

I am going to spin around with an O face
and learn how to whistle while I cum.
All the spilled semen will collect
into a halo above my head as though
sex will lead me to the divine,
to the secrets of the universe.

XVIII: 52 Weeks

The one time my heart has been owned
by another, I would find myself lucky
to see him once a week, and luckier still
to receive the gifts shot out of his cock
on those visits. My heart has been my own
for a while now, I think. It's mine.

Perhaps the way to glue myself back together,
to gather the plaster needed to fill the cracks
I no longer care to keep open, is to fuel
my cum-addiction at least once a week.
I'll find a man on an app or a date,
and I'll engulf him, his desire, and his love.

I'll cuddle against my pillows in my own bed
in my own room, content as my stomach or
my ass churns up the sloshing loads I pulled
out of a man who found me, *me*, so desirable.
The white will leak into my veins, and I will become
– Get it? Become, be cum. I laughed.

My dreams will cease being anything too heavy
to jot down in a collection of sexy poems.
I'll float through orgies and meet porn stars
who somehow know my name. I'll snap my fingers
and do a magic trick that summons a fountain
of precum. I'll wake with giggling morning wood.

Resolutions

Slip into my DMs, baby. Tell me how 52 weeks
is not near enough time to fill me with all
of your need. Tell me you long to fill a pool,
a sea, an ocean with your cum so that
I might be your world with my land
floating on your waters I chose to take.

XIX: Compliments

There are plenty of cocks, pecs, feet, and asses
on my social media feeds that I find beautiful,
the sorts of sculpted flesh that would cause
Michelangelo to fill an entire museum.

They get a like out of me, and I continue my scroll.
Afterall, most porn-posters get deluged
with compliments, and it's not like they need
another good boy wagging his tail at their heels.

What a silly thing to restrain oneself for. I'm scared
of annoying someone by calling them beautiful
when they're posting in a way declaring their body
is art? It is art, and they should know it.

Being a reply-guy is only embarrassing
if you're expecting something, anything,
if you've devolved into parasociality.
My chosen role is sweet. So it's what I'll be.

Tell the man with the fuzzy ass
that you'd love to camp in his forest.
Tell the foot dom with massive meaty soles
that if you were a tiny, you too would worship him.

*The sounds you made when he facefucked you
were really beautiful, you know. It was like
the building of Ticheli's music before the burst
of Vesuvius or something like that.*

Resolutions

I know this is a pit pic, but wow, it shows off your eyes. I'll tell him the hair on his chest seems like a wonderful place to nap. I'll say how I laughed at the TikTok-style porn skit.

The character I have carefully built for myself is sweet. To hell with nerves and awkwardness. To hell if they don't give a damn. The world can suck, but I suck better. So it's time I say what I mean.

Micky Omega

XX: Please Me

\Adrenaline junkies chase thrills
so they do stupid shit like leap
from cliffs into distant waters.

I'm like that but for pleasure giving,
so I do stupid shit like worship dick
and go home to make myself cum.

If I am going to learn how to be
in my body, then I need to learn
how to embrace being pleased.

So tonight, you're going to eat
me, dig your tongue into my hole
while I squirm and gasp at the strange feeling.

I'm going to cum tonight, and it won't
be at my own hand with my tongue
somewhere lapping at your skin.

I'm going to bask in the smooth wet
of a mouth working up and down my length,
spit soaking my trimmed brown bush.

Kiss my feet while you fuck me,
and if you finish first and can't go another thrust,
replace your erection with your fingers.

Resolutions

I am going to learn how to get milked,
how to melt into sheets with fingers
clutching at the silk as I moan.

I'm not going home to jack myself off.
No more selfish tops for me.
Make me whine, baby. Finish me off.

Micky Omega

XXI: Face Card

When someone says they wear masks in a poem,
you're going to assume it's metaphorical because
language is always supposed to be playing artful
tricks, but I've quite literally been wearing masks
in my porn, these little ski-cover slips of elastic,
black, blue, and white. This way I can post my cock
in peace without fear that it will come back to me.

Wouldn't it be bad if my family knew about what
a filthy little cum slut I am? Wouldn't it hurt my career
to be connected to my little snippets of erotica?
To the pen names of kinks that make people knit
their brows and widen their eyes in that way you do
when a movie reveals itself to be a stealth horror
about 45 minutes into the runtime…?

I am tired, you know. OnlyFans, prudish censorious
morons that they are, don't want you to talk about
tiredness. But it's exhausting to don a mask, you know?
Cloth gets heavy when you wear it to hide the mole
by your lip, the one on your ear, those details
you might be known by. There are bags under my eyes.
Damn, this is a sexy poem, isn't it? Great job, Micky.

I ought to tear away the cloth. Let them see my face.
I have a cute face. Fuck, the way I blush, how my eyes
shimmer with a begging need for a kiss when I'm getting
fucked by a cock that makes my eyes water? My face card
is worth something. I'm cute. I have a face that makes men
tell me how they want to see my lips bruised, stretched, and
dripping around their cocks, blue eyes staring up with longing.

Resolutions

Why am I embarrassed of sex? What am I scared of?
I think sex is art. Most porn creators don't go as far as I do
in waxing goddamn poetic about the cinematic value
of a pink tongue swirling around a pink hole in close-up.
They call themselves *content creators*. I hate that fucking term.
No, baby. You're actors. You're models and photographers.
You're writers, directors, musicians, and artists.

It's scary to be nude, isn't it? The fear is part of the excitement.
When you post, the eyes of strangers are on you. See, in art
you're supposed to kill your darlings, but in porn, you're part
of the art, so it's harder, different… Right? Right? I don't think
so. I am no less scared to be seen under my legal name
than to have my body judged under this stage name, this
naked drag persona that reveals my real desire for constant
cock.

More people would read my erotica if I advertised it
with my actual face, if I sat fully clothed and reading
all the taboo and tantalizing things in my cute little voice
that's neither masculine nor feminine but simply is.
More men would flirt with me. They'd join me in my
art-making crusade in this world of amateur pornography.
If the world is ending, why would you ever hide your face?

I am going to remove the cloth from my nose.
Maybe I need someone to press their fingers
underneath the hood, stretching, dancing over
my cheeks and my ears. It would be easier.
But even alone, I must be nude, truly nude,
for the first time. I have bills to pay, monetary and metaphoric,
and my face card has some credit to spend.

Micky Omega

XXII: Eating Ass

Here's the thing: If I'm going to learn
how to make a man squirm and moan
and cum from only his ass and only
my tongue dancing like a Degas portrait
all around the ballet stage of his ass,
then I'm going to need a good teacher.

So put a pillow under my head, lay me
down on your bed, and fire up a TV show
you've been meaning to catch up on
while you stretch your cheeks over mine
like my face might sink inside you and me
and my tongue become your favorite dildo.

XXIII: Gayer

You probably shouldn't talk
about nightmares in a sexy
way; Amazon and Smashwords,
OnlyFans and Just.forFans
don't like the shit. Heck,
even the mention of sleep
gets on their nerves.

I am scared for my country,
for the future of fucking,
and it seems like I'm not
alone. The nightmare
is contagious through
the web. How many
will quit porn this year?

I'm tempted to act out,
to show my face twisted
and contorted in the throes
of pleasure that comes
when a man impales me
on his cock stretching up
to my chest and mouth.

Nightmares can only be chased
away by posting self-portraits
painted in splattered white
dripping down the soft curves
of my face. I want a good

Micky Omega

night's sleep in my future
husband/owner's arms.

So tomorrow I shall wake
gayer than I am today.
I'm going to post videos
of me rocking the sax
with my cock both in the air
and behind a metal cage
as I play *Freebird*.

During the first Trump
administration, I went to my first
pride event, and I was called
the f-slur on my walk home.
The nightmare is a wet dream, now.
Some men I trust call me a *good fag*
while they lovingly dump their load.

The haters are going to search my name
and my face. They'll come across
my nude form getting fucked on screen,
bubble butt shaking like gelatin,
and then they'll come across their screens.
If we dream up a nightmare, then let's film
the gayest fucking orgy as an act of resistance.

XXIV: Orgy

Don't get me much for my birthday this year.
All I ask for is an empty room filled with
fresh smell-'em-ups and gentle LED lights,
walls lined with water, snacks, and energy drinks,
fluffy white towels piled up in the corner,
and a legion of men mingling together.

The windows ought to vibrate with the chorus
of moans and whimpers and chanted dirty talk.
Fog should paint the glass from all the hot breaths.
Can the hardwood floors transform into a slip-'n'-slide
slick with sweat, spit, and cum leaking out and over
all the birthday clowns initiating me to their ways.

XXV: Parody

If there's one thing the world is running low on,
it's submissive gay pups taking classical pieces
from Mozart, Beethoven, and other dudes
well in the public domain and transforming them
into pieces about sucking and fucking and cum.

Moonlight Sonata becomes the Cumshot Sonata.
Ode to Joy is Ode to Cock because happiness
is the same thing as a man's fuck stick, honestly.
Mozart has that piece, Lick Me in the Arse,
and I that one probably doesn't need much change.

Sabrina Carpenter is proof that the people long
for short people singing about how we adore sex.
I'm not much of a singer, but I do like being dumb
and horny and making music. So I'll set up
my microphone, treat it like a cock, and sing.

XXVI: Skirt

A little plaid mini-skirt
hanging off the waist
of a man with satyr-legs
and a jungle ass under
a fur-coated stomach
and over an always
hard five incher
sounds kind of hot,
doesn't it? It's the contrast
between the dainty femboy fit
and the hairy non-femboy
donning it. Gap-moe,
you might call it,
the cuteness of contradictions.
I want to be cute,
so the skirt is in my cart.

XXVII: Shaving

Standing in the shower,
monsoon on my back, I'll
tremble when he glides the razor
down the bubble of my butt. I'll
whimper when he presses
right against my hole. It's
sex the way he pulls my
cock up to the left and
trims my pubes, expose my
sack into the cooling
air, the wet spilled from his
tongue. Is this romance or
is such gentle giving in some
higher form of sex? Oh,
babe, I'm close, I'm close, I'm…

XXVIII: Cosplay

There's always a superhero online
showing off the thick bulge of lycra.
It takes super strength to lug around
such a heavy slab of man meat.

Isn't it every guy's dream to sleep
with Clark Kent? A soft top
is my kryptonite. Lift me up and
fuck me in the hall. Bend me like steal.

Or, shoot, the dorky jokes of Spider-man?
I'll sign up to be on the business end
of his web shooters any day of the week.
We could kiss each other upside down.

Before the next new year comes crashing
in through buildings like a villain
getting thrown, I'm going to fuck
a man dressed like a superhero.

I'll be the civilian he just saved
who wants to repay him.
I'll be the villain he teaches
how to be good with his cock.

Micky Omega

I'll wear whatever costume you want,
stud muffin. So order your supersuit
and flex your guns. Pop your pecs
and shake your shelf of an ass.

I'm going to be saved tonight
in the ecstasy of your kiss against mine,
our tongues battling for the fate of the cosmos
while our cocks leak through our clothes.

XXIX: DMs

I'm going to *Howdy handsome*
my way into gooning on a porn star's
throbbing cock while he turns my ass
into a punching bag for his thrusting hips.

Maybe we'll post about it online,
film the electricity shooting between
out intertwined legs as we slow kiss
with slow hands exploring hard backs.

I'll slip into his DMs the way he'll slip
deep inside my ass with my fingers
pressed hard into his shoulder blades,
gasping against his sweet neck.

I'm friends with a kinky dom
who landed himself a loving relationship
like this, dropping in on some cutie's inbox.
Surely it works the other way around, too.

Am I going to find the love of my life
or the fuck of my life? Both work.
So watch out boys, this cutie is prowling
for sweet, loving, indecent fucks.

Micky Omega

XXX: Vanilla

Around the world in 80 days
to seek out sweet and novel tastes
could almost lose inside the chase
the love of how vanilla lays
across the tongue in gentle ways.

I would trade every burning kink and thrill
for the consistent love we made on your bed
in missionary in the morning with us taking
turns holding my legs up while you rubbed
your uncut length inside me, that cock
of yours which has yet to be beat by any other.
You would call me beautiful before I reached up
and wrapped my arms around your head
for a kiss. Your slight belly would rub against
my own never-softening cock. Sometimes,
you couldn't cum, but you'd fuck me
until I did. I never lasted long
in your lubed up hand.
I've had more wild,
more memorable
encounters filled with kink and cum.
But I still think of you and your vanilla skin
when I fuck myself alone at night.

Around the world in 80 nights,
remember how you loved the plain old lights.
Submissiveness feels oh so right,
but then again, so was his simple sight.

Resolutions

XXXI: Doggy Style

It'd be funny to title a poem "Doggy Style"
and have it be about pup play alone
and not the sexual position.

Sometimes it's fun to disappoint people,
like when I'm told my ass is too tight
for a man to even put the tip in.

I like riding and missionary. I like positions
made for easy kissing. I've got this thing,
an oral fixation? Kiss me or I feel bad.

I want to be a better bottom. I want to find
more pleasure in the world because there's
enough stress and pain in it.

Get me on all fours and put your weight
on my back. Together, we can teach me
how to take it doggy style.

I want to moan. I want to cry in a good way.
I don't want to grimace when a top likes
pounding me from behind.

Micky Omega

My behind is beautiful, or so I've been told.
Pretty things like my ass should feel good.
I want to feel good. So fuck me and teach me

how to take an animalistic breeding
how to love new positions
how to cum without a kiss

XXXII: Pits

There's something about man musk,
about the way it makes your head
go all fuzzy and your spine tingle
and your cock harden, how it sends
you straight into that subby space
where you whimper and hump his thighs
while you huff and burrow your way
deeper and deeper under his arms,
tongue flicking out and hoping he doesn't
taste of deodorant, that chalky chemical
that has a way of clinging to the mouth.

Or is it just me? Am I the only one
who wants a sort of stinky man
to clean his pits each night
with my mouth? For him
to hold my head against
his warm flesh and evaporate
my nerves in his intoxicating scent
until I drift off to sleep engulfed by him,
to journey into dreams laced with his musk

XXXIII: Punishment

Sometimes being a good boy
means being a little shit.

It means disobeying.
It means being a brat.
It means stumbling into spankings.
It means drawing out degradation.

It means giving him a reason to play
the part of the disciplinarian
who needs to teach his boy
what it means to be a bad boy
and how to turn good again.

Dear God, how I want to be a good boy.
I've never been Catholic but I've got
this whole Catholic guilt-daddy issues thing
that makes me want to dress up in priest's robes
and worship a holy vampire who'll grab my neck,
toss me into a gentle hell, and then forgive me.

Forgive me, sir. I want to be forgiven.
Let me be your good boy again.
Fuck the sin out of me on the church pews
pushed together to make our bed.
I'll beg to quench my thirst
with your holy water.

XXXIV: Grand Canyon

Let's fuck in your car in the passenger seat
parked somewhere with a great goddamn view.

Control my hips and flood my Grand Canyon
as I look out at the acres of stars.

You can really see the beauty of creation out here,
but the only heaven I believe in is way you fuck me.

Spin me around, baby. Let me look at your face
and take in another wonder of the earth.

Your eyes, baby. Your eyes. I'll stare in them
until we melt into your seats.

It's your turn next. I'm nice and hard for you.
I'm always hard when I'm with you.

Sit on my cock and look out at the view.
Let's flipfuck with this view 'til the end of time.

Micky Omega

XXXV: Nudes

Take a pic every morning
of the Babel Tower of my cock.

Set up a sexy, masturbating shoot
with costumes at least once a month.

Figure out the best angles
to show off my pink, hairy hole.

Show off my feet for all my fellow
good little submissive bitches.

Record my showers and workouts.
Chat to the camera while jerking off.

I want to decorate my body
and accept the fear of nudity.

Take more nudes and plaster them
in art museums in my phone.

Art patrons will lines up
to tell me I'm a beautiful subject.

Resolutions

They'll say my lips would look
even better wrapped around their cocks.

They'd say my tight boy pussy
looks like it needs to be coated in cum.

They'd sing about how my cock
should be buried in their throats like theirs in mine.

There's no time to spend life clothed.
I'll take the nudes so someone wants me.

Micky Omega

XXXVI: Throat Fuck

I'm jealous of those guys who can lay down
on a mattress with their heads hanging
off the side, upside down, mouths open
and throats relaxed for a big dicked
alpha male type to fuck their thrussies
with wild abandon like they've got an ass
for a face, a thing that can take a real pounding.

See, I really love balls. They get a bad rap
in mainstream media, but my happy place
is with a loose sack on my lips. So these
throat fuckees who get to suck cock
with churning nuts hitting their noses and eyes
are really and truly living the dream.
It's why I like 69-ing lying under someone.

My favorite porn actors on social media
are the handsome dorky men who love
to fuck a throat. They hold their boys down
as they gag and squirm happily on their cocks.
They laugh and tell men they're prettiest
with slime spilling over their face and cum
deep inside their hungry, greedy gullets.

Resolutions

I wanna squelch and belch with a sweet sack
bouncing on my nose. I wanna look up
and see a top's pretty ass and have the stamina
to ask him to turn around and sit on my wet face
so I can eat him out until he's hard again
and ready to fuck my throat all over.
Someone teach me how to suck.

XXXVII: Painting

I want to be a work of art,
a walking performance piece
so thoroughly coated in the spilling
slop of thick and viscous semen
that I'm a creature walking gay out
the blue white lagoon.

It'll be like I'm wearing a wedding suit
of ivory white, tailored to my form
and sewn with the seeds of my lover
who probably scared off his exes
with the sheer volume that geysers
out his faithful fuck stick.

Coat my face. Paint my chest.
Let me walk the runway
with a beautiful pearl necklace
and a tail of diamonds leakings
down my legs. I don't want an inch
of my skin to go without knowing
the warmth of your loads.

XXXVIII: Poetry

Wouldn't it be funny to be the Rupi Kaur
of filthy gay fucking? The viral Instagram
poet of normie fujoshis who really like
seeing gay guys moaning while they kiss
and fill each other with their cocks.

Like yeah, share my TikTok sex sintesi skits.
Post my erotic stanzas under photos
of your OTPs and cafe coffees.

I'm long-winded, everyone knows.
The only way to shut me up
is to put my mouth to use,
so I need to write poetry
while kissing a man's
large, soft feet.

That way I'll get to the point quickly,
and by that I mean putting the laptop away
and getting that round pointy tip
of his handsome leaking cock in my mouth.

XXXIX: Role Play

A doctor is going to walk in and conduct
a physical like a maestro who knows
how to make his patients whimper.

A dentist is going to need to do a deep
gum check by sticking an instrument
far down my cavernous throat.

I'm going to visit my professor
and take in an in-depth lesson
on the philosophies of submission.

A wizard is going to summon an incubus
to teach him all the wild ways
of healing sex magic.

I'll break out my saxophone
and give a personal concert
to my handsome benefactor.

I want to live so many lives
and have them each find
the ancient beauty of sex.

XL: I Love You

I'm the type to say *I love you*
in bed because I am grateful
for this moment where our flesh
becomes one rippling with pleasure.

I've been swallowing my tongue
while men fuck me instead of cum
like I'd really want. I can't wait
until I can utter those words again.

Fuck me. I love you.
Fuck me. I love you.
Cum, baby. I love you.
Breed me deep 'cause I love you.

XLI: I Hate You

Isn't it kind of hot to think there's someone
out there who's you're mortal enemy
who can't help but pushing you
against a wall with a fierce unending kiss
while you're both tearing off each other's clothes?

Like sure, in real life, that'd be toxic,
like two exes who never *really* fall out of love
and end up tumbling in each other's beds
for the rest of their lives. It's probably better
in movies. But it's hot to think about.

Imagine the passion. Imagine how hot
someone has to find you that hate
turns horny. It'd be a competition
to make the other person feel amazing
because how embarrassing would that be?

I don't want to make any enemies,
so I guess we'll have to pretend.
Don't hold it against me, baby.
I hate you. Fuck me now.
I hate you. Make me your bitch.

XLII: Swing

I like playing swing notes.
They're the dance of jazz.
What would it be like to lay
in a sex swing and have someone
play my ass like it's the most
romantic jazz tune ever made?

Micky Omega

XLIII: Step on Me

Look, I think feet are hot.
I mean, not generally;
I don't want to fuck them
or anything like that.

But I'm a submissive
good boy type, so I like
kissing them. I like their warmth.
I like the feel against my skin.

Turn me into a mountain
with my hole as the summit
for you to climb to and mount
with your foot pressed on my face.

Step on me. I want to be put
in my place, sir. Get your rocks off
in the mountain while your toes
brush over my lips.

XLIV: Holidays

I tend to spend celebratory days alone,
so this year my pipe dream goal
is to have a horny holiday
where fireworks are released
in electric kisses and exploding
bursts of cum like Christmas crackers.

Let's celebrate in my bed.
We can show off our cuddling pile
on all of our socials while we sing
songs about snogging and sucking
and not being alone.

Micky Omega

XLV: Toys

I'm going to lay you down on the mattress
with a pristine fluffy pillow holding your face
and silk sheets under your skin to spread out
over with your stretching, gasping limbs,
chest down and fingers digging into the bed.

I'm going to dig my tips, finger and tongue,
against the spread of your divine back,
those broad shoulders that spend days
protecting me as if I need protecting
finally relaxing with the sighs you spill.

I'm going to twist the cool metal
of the small buttplug with a sapphire base
in and out of your gentle, hardworking hole
until it's popping out of you with ease
and you're ready for a synthetic cock.

I'm going to kiss your thighs while you moan
and squirm, hole puckering, back arching,
pushing back against the dildo each time
I pull it out of you. It won't be long before
you're begging me to get you pregnant.

I'm going to flip you on your back and place
your weary feet on my lips, tongue flicking
between your toes as I finally sink inside
your slippery depths. When I'm balls deep,
I'm going to slip a pocket pussy on your cock.

Resolutions

I'm going to thrust into you with the gentle,
animalistic thunder of a man who wants
to make love and breed another man,
with each rock of my hips plunging you
into the silicon toy wrapped around your dick.

I'm going to fuck you until you fill the onahole
and then I'm going to fuck you some more
until you're filled with my seed. I'll stop it
from spilling out by putting that sapphire
plug back inside you. You're gonna get pregnant.

Micky Omega

XLVI: Cinema

Let's rent out a room in the cinema
so this sex tape we're about to make
can get the Cannes Festival moment
it's going to deserve, even if the only
Palm d'Or it'll get is the sloppy palming
we'll give each other's pre-cum spilling
beautiful cocks as we relive our hours
spent together in those rooms and witness
the glory of your money shot on the big screen.

XLVII: Laundry

Put me in a crate
lined with your laundry,
your gym clothes stained
with sweat and precum,
your socks and shirts and jocks
for me to make a nest out of
while you get to work or
cook us dinner.

When you open up
the door, I'll smell
like you, and immediately
I'll go in for a million kisses,
for sniffs directly from the source.
Your pheromones drive me wild.
When I go home, send me
with one of your shirts to cuddle
and another to cum in
night after night
until I'm back in your arms.

Micky Omega

XLVIII: Nipples

Guys love it when I swirl my tongue
around the ice cream dollops
of their nipples standing pert
on their chests.

Don't get me wrong,
I love that shit. I like
chest hair against my nose.
I like making men squirm.

I love it when a guy presses
his hand to the back of my head
and holds me still on one nipple
then guides me over to the other.

But, like, I don't get it.
A tongue on my chest is…
fine. It's fine. Nothing special.
How do you get to that pleasure?

This year I'm going to lean
against my bedroom wall
tweaking my nipples between
gentle pinching fingers.

Resolutions

Maybe ice cubes
will do the trick,
melting against my flesh
in slow and tiny circles.

I'll get some nipple clamps
with pretty chains dangling
from them, and wear them
to the club like jewelry.

I want to say I've learned
how to enjoy every inch
of my body. I want to understand
the pleasure of a tongue on my chest.

XLIX: Mirror

This hot military dude I like
to suck off likes to sit
in a computer chair in front
of a mirror so he can goon
in my mouth to the sight
of his masculinity dominating
a good boy who whimpers
and slobbers all over him.

All the hot social media
gays who post with their
chiseled cocks on display
have those skinny floor length
mirrors that they post at least
once splattered all over
with their leaking cum
that I really rather
went on my face.

So I'm going to jerk off
while scanning my form
in my bedroom mirror,
in the one in the bathroom,
while filming myself
in selfie mode
until I too find it hot
to see how pleasure

Resolutions

crosses my face
curls my toes
trembles my brows
shakes my moans

Splat! on the mirror
Splat! on my stomach
Splat! on my face
I am a good boy
I am pretty
I am handsome
I am sexy
I am sex

Micky Omega

L: Resolutions

Ambition is the sexiest trait a man
can have, apparently, though that
sounds like utter bullshit to me.
The sexiest thing a man can be
is a dork. Get me a a guy who's
going to pause the movie to go
on a rant about some behind-the-scenes
fact over a workaholic ladder climber
any day. I'll ladder climb onto
a dork's dick. That's besides the point.

Ambition is a good thing to have.
There's a reason we make resolutions
every turn of a new year. We need
something to strive for. It makes the new
feel less scary and way more sexy.
It makes us feel sexy. I want men
to find me sexy, so I've laid out
49 horny resolutions for this year
with hopes to achieve them all.

Ambition is a dream to transform
pornographic perception to acclaim,
to push down prudes and puritans
and celebrate the art of the erotic,
of the poetry in dirty talk, of the cinema
in a well-placed cum shot, of the Picasso
in a penis pic. Sex does not make
art no longer art. Fill the museums.

Resolutions

Ambition is envisioning my body
as brick and mortar, as a hotel for men,
as a home for my future husband,
as a bank collecting donations of sperm,
as a greenhouse nursery turning seed
into life and holy creation, as a church
where I can worship the mundane divine.

Ambition is dreaming that you
are so worthy of pleasure
that you might find ecstasy
in so many strange spots
that you might find joy
down every corner.

Ambition is telling a man exactly
what I want, how I long to be treated,
how I want to make him feel good
and how he's going to please me
while also declaring my boundaries.

Ambitions is the grit of teeth and
the deep breaths of pushing your limits
with a free and enthusiastic will
so you can take more pleasure tomorrow.

Micky Omega

Ambition is the endeavor to exist
in this dark and often cruel world
and be a creature of shining sweetness.

Ambition is the strive I have to be
a good boy for a handsome man.

Ambition is making me cum.

About the Author

Micky Omega is a gay adult performer and erotica author who wants to celebrate and explore every corner of desire, no matter the weird corners to which it might extend. This good boy loves submission, poetry, and music.

www.ingramcontent.com/pod-product-compliance
Ingram Content Group UK Ltd.
Pitfield, Milton Keynes, MK11 3LW, UK
UKHW040002311224
452994UK00001B/144